THE PORTEOUS RIOT

by

Robert McNeil

Scotland's Cultural Heritage
ISBN0 907692 42 7

Acknowledgements

The author would like to thank the staffs of the Edinburgh Room and Scottish Library (Central Public Library), the Scottish Record Office, the National Library of Scotland Manuscripts Room, and the ever-helpful Mr. Arnott Wilson of Edinburgh City Archives.

Fiona McIntyre of Scotland's Cultural Heritage contributed additional research, and James Gilhooley suggested useful detail. The text was read by Professor Harry Dickinson of the University's History Department, though any mistakes or opinions are solely the author's.

The Scotland's Cultural Heritage staff who worked on this book were:–

Art Direction	**Jon Dalrymple**
Graphics	**Mike Walker**
Cover Design:	**Michèle Paterson**
Photography:	**Fred Vance**
Typing:	**Mandy Elliot, Aly Meiklejohn**
Typesetting:	**Jonathan Galtry**

Printed by Drummond Street Reprographics Unit

Scotland's Cultural Heritage is funded by the Manpower Services Commission's Community Programme

Cover:	Execution in the Grassmarket (from an etching by Skene)

"It was a fatal weary Night,
When ye conveen'd me to affright,
Baith sad and driry was my Plight,
When ye broke in with main and might,
And on me seiz'd;
Baith grim and ghastly was your Sight,
It not me pleas'd."
(*'Captain Porteous's Ghost', Anon., 1738)*

"But oh! what dark'ning Colours shall display
The aggravated Horrors of the Day,
When one Man's Madness, in a moment, hurl'd
Numbers from Health from Life, and from the World."
(*'A Poem, occasioned by the Death of the Persons unfortunately killed... after the Execution of Andrew Wilson', Anon., 1736?)*

1. THE FIFE SMUGGLERS

On the morning of 9 January 1736, Andrew Wilson, George Robertson and William Hall sailed across the Forth from Leith to Kinghorn. Had there been "passports" in those days, Wilson's occupation may have been recorded as "baker in Pathhead, near Kirkcaldy", Robertson's as "stabler in Bristo", and Hall's, more vaguely, as "inndweller in Edinburgh". They could not after all have given their true occupations : smugglers.

Wilson was the most dedicated and successful of these, but of late his fortunes had been at a low ebb, having suffered many confiscations and penalties at the hands of the revenue officers. Now he had hit on a plan to get his own back and that plan was simple and to the point: he would rob the Excise man directly.

At Kinghorn, he and his companions hired horses and rode in the evening to Anstruther Easter, where they had supper before walking on to Pittenweem. At Pitteweem there was an ale-house owned by the Widow Fowler. Here, the three men drank brandy and ale, and when Wilson proposed an illicit deal with some casks of brandy, the Widow Fowler warned him to be quiet because James Stark, the Collector of Excise, was resting upstairs. "Is he now?" said Wilson.

Next thing, while Robertson pulled out a cutlass and guarded the door, Wilson and Hall dashed up the stairs. They beat on the Collector's door, apparently shouting "Murder the dogs and burn the house"[1], and, with the mistress and maid of the house crying and screaming, Collector Stark fled via the window, taking a bag of money with him, but alas forgetting his breeches. These contained a purse with $52^1/_2$ guineas, a pocket-book with £140 in bank notes, and six or seven pounds in silver. Wilson and Hall grabbed these, along with a Bible, pen-knife, silver shoe-buckles, a seal, and a pair of pistols.

In the meantime, Alexander Clerk, another Excise man lodged in the room next to Stark's, had also fled via the window and, having remembered his breeches, felt no inhibitions about running to get help. (Collector Stark himself, minus his breeches, lay under some straw in the yard until four o'clock in the morning).

Robertson, after heading off some curious locals by taking them elsewhere for a drink, later met up with Wilson in Anstruther Easter. Hall was not so fortunate. He was chased by some soldiers whom Clerk had alerted, and a sergeant with a halberd expertly hooked him in by the scruff of the neck. Hoping for a pardon, Hall told them everything: where he had dropped the purse - "in a furr near a dunghill" — and where his companions could be found. Found they duly were — in bed, pretending to be asleep. The three misadventurers were then sent to Edinburgh's Tolbooth prison, which Sir Walter Scott described as "gloomy and haggard in aspect, its black stanchioned windows opening through its dingy walls like the apertures of a hearse". On the wall of the main prison hall was the legend:

'A prison is a house of care,
A place where none can thrive,
A touchstone true to try a friend,
A grave for men alive.'

Here, prisoners came under the care of the Town Guard and its Captain, John Porteous.

2. CAPTAIN PORTEOUS OF THE GUARD.

The Town Guard was an armed militia, employed to keep the peace in the city. Its origins lay in the sixteenth century, after the defeat at Flodden, when citizens were chosen to 'watch' for invaders. In 1648, a force of 60 men and one Captain was formally set up, that force being increased in 1682 to 108 plus sergeants and officers. In 1736, it comprised about 100 men plus three Captain-lieutenants. The Town Guard uniform was a dull red coat, black cocked hat edged with white braiding and black buckled shoes, and their weapons were the musket and the Lochaber axe (a slim hooked axe on a long wooden pole). Their H.Q. was the City Guard-house, a one-storey building near the Tron Church. The poet, Robert Fergusson, described it as "a lumbersome an' stinkin' biggin".

Most soldiers in the Town Guard normally worked on at their trades, only turning out when need be, and many were Gaelic-speaking, ex-army Highlanders. The townspeople, especially the young, called them the 'Town Rats' and liked to throw stones at them on the King's birthday.

Into this outfit John Porteous first came as an ensign in 1718, after a spell as drill-master to the Train-bands (volunteers mustered to defend the city against the 1715 Jacobite rebellion). Prior to this, he had served in Flanders, where it is said that he murdered his captain, but that is perhaps just one of the many apocryphal tales concerning the man. In 1726 he himself became a Captain-lieutenant of the Town Guard and, soon, the most reviled individual in the town.

What sort of a man, then, was this Porteous? Accounts from the time are biased against him, the most comprehensive being *The Life and Death of Captain John Porteous*, published in 1737, which William Roughead counsels, is "so violently partial as to defeat its own design."[2] Nevertheless, the anonymous author's physical description of Porteous has perhaps some basis in truth: "He was of a middle Size, broad-shoulder'd, strong-limb'd, short-necked, his Face a little pitted with the Small-Pox and round; his looks mild and gentle, his Features having nothing of the Fierce or Brutal; his Eyes languid, not quick and sprightly, and his Complexion upon the Brown. His outward Appearance answer'd not his Inside."

Reputedly, he beat his parents: "when he was check'd by his Father, in his vicious Carreer, he almost put the good old Man to Death, by Kicks and Blows." He beat his wife: "He often dragg'd her out of Bed by the Hair of her Head, and beat her to the Effusion of her Blood . . . He did Things to her, which I am asham'd to write, and you would blush to read. All this was done because she stood in the way of his adulterous Embraces with her Maids." He beat his men: "seldom a Day past but some one or other of his Squade felt the Weight of his Stick".

But, above all, he beat 'the mob', the common people, whom he, a tailor's son, despised: "these People were sure of a Beating from him. The Hatred and Terror of him increased every Year, and his Character of wicked Debauche was known to every Body so that he was universally hated and feared by the lower Set of People".

The gentry, on the other hand, seemed to accept him, and with them he sought to insinuate himself, particularly through indulging the fashionable passion for golf, at which he could disport himself like a gentleman.

We can supplement, if not balance, this portrait of Porteous from the historical record. We know, for example, that on 7 September 1716, less than a year after his initial appointment as drill-master to the Train-bands, he was temporarily dismissed for some unknown misdemeanour; that his appointment as Captain in 1726 was not uniformly approved of by the magistrates (the town councillors); that, in March 1732, he reacted with savagery in quelling a skirmish over the appointment of a minister at West Kirk; and that in July 1735, he and another Captain, John Fergusson, were dismissed from their commands, after fighting with each other in the presence of the Town Council magistrates.[3]

On the other hand, we know that he gave money to the subscription for the first infirmary in the town but, even here, we are constrained to note that having one's name on such a subscription list, along with the aristocrats and important citizens of the day, was a valuable social cachet.[4]

Perhaps the redoubtable Roughead has given us the best picture of Porteous, in which he might be found "gossiping with his cronies at the Cross in

The City Guard

the open-air club of Auld Reekie, exchanging news and snuff-boxes... or swinging his cane as he swaggered down the High Street to the Guard-house, with a keen eye for a comely face in a piquant plaid or swinging sedan, proudly indifferent to the menaces of the herd... Fond of his glass and its proverbial concomitant; ruffling it with the best or worst in that free-living, tavern-haunting society of eighteenth-century Auld Reekie; carrying himself with a high head and a hard hand; equally ready to assert his dignity with oath or cane; arrogant, rash, intemperate; very jealous for his prerogative of office... In a rough, rude age, dealing with a mob whose excesses far outvie any performances of our own policed proletariat, it may well be that so formidable an officer was a civic necessity."[5]

To just what excesses that civic necessity could lead him we shall soon see.

3. AN ESCAPE, A HANGING AND A MASSACRE

If, in eighteenth-century Edinburgh, the Town Guard was too often the object of ridicule (and Porteous in particular the object of hatred), then smugglers were the object of popular admiration. In the wake of the Union with England, the new revenue laws (hitherto little known in Scotland) were strongly resented, causing riots and elevating smuggling to the status of a national sport. In their own communities, smugglers were heroes, with a strong bedrock of support amongst those who enjoyed tea, tobacco or brandy at bargain prices.

So, when the Pittenweem Three — Wilson, Hall and Robertson — came up for trial on 2 March 1736, popular sympathy was more with them than with the Excise man who had been robbed of his money-laden breeches. The charges were 'Stouthrieff, Housebreaking and Robbery' and, since stouthrieff also meant robbery (but particularly with violence), there was some initial quibbling about the nature of the charges. No amount of quibbling, however, could belie the guilt of the defendants. The defence tried to argue that the three were in Fife on legitimate business, that they had drank too much at Widow Fowler's and, in sum, "if it was done by them, they were drawn into it suddenly and occasionally, being very drunk, and had not time to come to themselves".[6] The prosecution brought forward 18 witnesses to prove that it was indeed 'done by them' and that drunkenness was no excuse. The jury agreed and unanimously pronounced the three guilty. That verdict was perhaps no surprise but the punishment was: all three were sentenced to be hanged on 14 April. Hall, having turned King's evidence and betrayed his comrades, later had his sentence commuted to transportation for life. Wilson and Robertson went back to the Tolbooth.

In the early hourse of Friday 9 April, Wilson, Robertson and two other prisoners tried a daring escape, using files and saws smuggled in by sympathisers (who, reportedly, dressed as women and sang psalms outside to cover the noise made by the sawing of the prison bars). One prisoner called Stewart successfully escaped, through the window and down three storeys by rope. Unfortunately, Wilson, a stout man, tried to go next and got wedged in the window, preventing the escape of his comrades behind him.

Two days later, Wilson and Robertson were taken to the Tolbooth Kirk in St. Giles to contemplate their sins before meeting their Maker, in three days' time. But, with the bells ringing and the righteous still arriving, the two desperadoes had other things on their minds. The *Caledonian Mercury* takes up the story:

"Wilson boldly attempted to break out by wrenching himself out of the hands of four armed soldiers. Finding himself disappointed here, his next care was to employ the soldiers till Robertson should escape; this he effected by securing two of them in his arms; and after calling out, GEORDIE, DO FOR THY LIFE! snatched hold of a third with his teeth. Hereupon Robertson, after tripping up the fourth, jumped out of the seat and ran over the top of the pews with incredible agility, the audience opening a way for him".[7]

It is significant that the 'righteous' did their best to let Robertson escape. He went to Holland. Wilson went back to the Tolbooth. His popularity with the people was now much enhanced and the taverns of the town buzzed with rumours that an attempt to rescue him would be made.

Next day, Monday the 12th, the Lord Provost ordered the Town Treasurer to provide the Town Guard with powder and shot. On the Tuesday, the hangman himself was ensconced in the Tolbooth under a heavy guard, lest he be kidnapped, and Porteous was sent with a letter to General Moyle, commander of the Forces in Scotland. The letter contained an unprecedented application for a 150-strong detachment of troops to be drawn up in the Lawnmarket on the execution-day. Porteous bitterly resented this, taking it as a slur on his own capacity to control the mob.

On the Wednesday, 14 April 1736, Porteous, apparently inflamed with wine, fetched Wilson from the Tolbooth. He forced him to wear wrist-manacles that were far too tight and, on the way to the Grassmarket, as he marched his prisoner past the detachment of reinforcements, his own foul mood only worsened.

In the Grassmarket itself, a huge crowd had gathered, every window in the high tenements nearby taken by "sightseers" who had paid well for the privilege. The crowd was sullen and quiet. No cheers or jeers, only grim expectation — an atmosphere as if thunder was due. The execution went ahead, nevertheless, and still the crowd did not move.

Only when the hangman, John Dalgleish, started ascending the ladder to cut down the body did trouble begin. It was the custom on these occasions for the two magistrates in attendance to witness the hanging and then adjourn to a nearby tavern for a somewhat ghoulish dinner known as the 'deid-chack'. After the body had hung half-an-hour, they would signal from the tavern window that it was to be taken down.

On this occasion, things went differently. According to Porteous's later deposition, after the body had hung for 'some time' (in reality, about fifteen minutes), some in the crowd shouted for it to be cut down.[8] Porteous, perhaps on edge, sent Town Officer Alexander Thomson to the magistrates and they sent word back that the body was to hang another fifteen minutes.[9] After just ten more minutes, however, the hangman took his first two or three steps up the ladder, only to be pelted with dirt and stones, one of which bloodied his nose. He came back down again, seeking the protection of the Town Guard.

Now, this stone-throwing was de rigeur for these occasions. "It is," as the author of *The Life and Death of Captain Porteous* pointed out, "ordinary for the rable [sic.] at Edinburgh, moved with the common sentiments of Humanity, upon such Occasions, without being able to comprehend the Ends of Society, to let fly Stones at the Hangman." What is more, witnesses would later testify that on this occasion there were in fact fewer stones thrown than usual.

After the initial stone-throwing, however, a section of the crowd pressed forward and someone cut down Wilson's body. More stones and dirt were thrown, this time hitting and injuring the Guard. With the attention of the Guard thus diverted, the corpse was then spirited away, the wishful idea being "to recover him to Life, by causing the veins of both Arms to be opened".[10]

What happened next is one of the greatest outrages ever committed on the streets of Edinburgh, and the following account is a reconstruction based on the statements of over 100 witnesses, the majority incriminating Porteous. Porteous, waving his gun threateningly, tried to push the crowd back. Still they pressed on. A stone hit him on the hip. He fired into the crowd, killing one young man. Then he ordered his reluctant men to fire, which they did, but over the heads of the crowd (thus hitting some spectators at the windows).

He cursed them and ordered them to level their muskets. They did. Two more people were killed, and several wounded.

The crowd retreated in panic and shock. Porteous gathered his men around him and marched them off towards the West Bow. Remnants of the crowd, whose fear had turned to anger, went in pursuit. Half-way up the steep incline, the soldiers of the Guard turned round and fired again. Three more people dropped down dead. Porteous led his men away from the carnage and down the Lawnmarket where in some disarray they stumbled past the impressive but bewildered regular troops who had been brought up in case there was trouble.

4. THE TRIAL OF CAPTAIN PORTEOUS

It was later claimed on Porteous's behalf that, back at the Guard-house, he prevented some of those who had fired from cleaning their guns.[11] From the Guard-house he did himself go straight to the Spread-Eagle tavern to see the Provost and magistrates who were there and immediately began denying that he had fired or ordered his men to fire. He had his own musket sent for and, upon inspection, it appeared not to have been fired.

He was then taken, followed by an angry crowd, to the Burgh Room and, after more formal enquiries, he was put into custody. Six more people were examined that day and, in the following week, statements were taken from a further eighty-four. Fifteen soldiers of the Town Guard were put into jail.

On 5 July, having come close to being torn apart by the mob outside, Porteous appeared at the High Court, where he was charged with having fired at the crowd, causing death and injury, and having ordered his men to do likewise. The prosecution brought forward 28 witnesses, 26 of whom had given statements at the 'precognition' (the preliminary examination held by the magistrates immediately after the events). The defence brought forward 18 witnesses, only two of whom had come forward at the precognition, one saying little or nothing.

The defence case was that: 1. The men had been given orders by the Provost to shoot if there was trouble; 2. The stones thrown at the Guard presented a threat to life; 3. The soldiers of the Guard were still smarting after Robertson's escape and so, despite Porteous's best efforts, were in a mood to fire; 4. Porteous, though employed for some years as "The Scourge of the Mob", was "never once known to proceed to extremities"[12]; 5. Porteous did not shout 'Fire!' — he shouted 'Do not fire!'; 6. A soldier stepped out from behind Porteous and fired the first shot, and Porteous tried to stop further firing; 7. His

Detail from The Porteus Mob by James Drummond

(By kind permission of the National Gallery of Scotland)

actions after the firing — marching the men off and reporting to the Provost - were not those of a guilty man.

We shall come to points 1, 2, 5 and 6 presently. Point 3 is possible, point 4 would have drawn laughter from the gallery, and point 7 is of little substance.

Nineteen of the prosecution witnesses, including the advocate Sir William Forbes and Mr. William Fraser, son of Lord Saltoun, positively saw Porteous fire; most of them added that his was the first shot fired. Of a further three, one heard him fire, one was almost certain that he fired, and one fairly certain. One agreed with the defence that it was a soldier stepping out from behind Porteous who fired first. Nine of the prosecution witnesses also heard Porteous order his men to fire, and one heard him mention the word 'fire'.[13]

For the defence, five witnesses — plus the prosecution witness already mentioned - said that a certain soldier stepped forward from the ranks behind Porteous and fired the first shot (see point 6 above). George Vint, for example, saw "one of the soldiers, a BLACK-HAIRED Man, step forward before the Pannel [i.e. the accused] and fire his Piece [i.e. his musket]". (Interestingly, the prosecution witness who supported the defence — the once and future Lord Provost, George Drummond - declared at the precognition that the soldier who stepped forward and fired had "CHESTNUT COLOURED HAIR". Whoever fired, the result was the same: a lad with "a Blew Bonnett and his own hair... dropt down dead by that shot and his brains were lying on the one side of his head").[14] A further two defence witnesses said Porteous did not fire, one did not see him fire, three saw two or more soldiers start the firing, two definitely did not hear Porteous order firing and two specifically heard him say not to fire.[15]

Because the cross-examinations were transcribed and recorded in third-person statements, some aspects of the case are not always clear to the modern researcher. For example, on the question of whose gun was used and when, "the statements", as Roughead has noted, "are very confusing."[16] It is not always clear whether witnesses are referring to the first shooting or the second.

Nonetheless, some of the accounts are vivid enough. William Johnstoun, for example, saw Porteous fire a gun taken from a soldier (that was why his own gun was clean, argued the prosecution), and "he appeared to be in Passion, and it was some short time before he was Master of the Gun". Prosecution witness, Andrew Daw, almost never lived to tell the tale: "the Pannel [i.e. Porteous]... fired his Piece toward the Place where the Deponent [i.e. witness] was standing; upon which a Baxter in the Abbey, called Charles

Husband, dropt just by the deponent; and his the Deponent's Coat was torne in the Shoulder with the same Shot".

Defence witness, George Smeiton, "saw a Man with a Silk Napkine about his Neck, press upon the Pannel [Porteous]... but a young Gentleman there, in green Cloaths, kept him off". One of the soldiers of the Guard, appearing for the defence, "heard the soldiers say, one to another, Fire, or we shall all be knockt down". At the precognition, William Murray, who had been "just under the gallows... within four or five yeards distance of Capt. Porteous", heard the Captain call to his men "Damnye for Buggars wont ye fire sharp shott".[17]

If we look now at points 1, 2 and 5 in the defence case (as enumerated above), taking them in reverse order, we find firstly that the notion of Porteous shouting "Don't fire!" is strongly contradicted by those who heard him shout "Fire!", accompanied by whatever form of cursing, and those who also heard him order his men to level their guns after they had fired into the air.

The question of how much danger the Guards were in is not so easily settled. The prosecution described the stone-throwing as "this triffling Provocation". At the precognition it was recorded that David Brown, employed to dismantle the scaffold, "has been witness to a great many executions of the like kind [but] he never saw so few stones thrown att any of them as att this".[18] Others testified similarly. On the other hand, two soldiers of the Guard suffered fractured shoulders, others were hit on the legs and the drummer was cut on the head and his drum smashed. Several witnesses testified that Porteous himself was hit on the hip by a stone.

As to the question of it all having been the Lord Provost's fault, an interesting sidelight on this later emerged concerning a Major Pool, of the Welsh Fusiliers, who had expressed the fear that the troops would be "insulted and abused, as they commonly are by the mob"[19], but he was reassured by the Provost that the Town Guard themselves would be given ammunition to fire at the mob's legs, if necessary. This detail, however, did not emerge at the trial, where it was argued by the prosecution that, whatever precautions had been arranged by the magistrates, they did not amount to an order for firing on the people.

Whatever the fine detail, the overwhelming feeling of the court was that Porteous had fired and had ordered his men to fire and, accordingly, he was found guilty by the jury and condemned to be hanged on 8 September.

5. REPRIEVE AND REVENGE

The people of Edinburgh were delighted with that verdict, but not everyone in Scotland was, least of all those powerful friends that Porteous had made on the golf course, and those, such as the Earl of Islay, who managed Scotland's affairs on London's behalf. They began a campaign for clemency, "conscience being more than a thousand witnesses"[20], and soon had a petition to that effect signed by fifty of the great and the good, including four Commissioners of Excise and one of Customs, one Duke, four Earls, one Viscount, four Baronets, two Sheriffs, two Colonels and a General. A veritable "Vermine of Villains", as one observer called them.[21]

The petition was presented to Queen Caroline (acting regent while George II was in Hanover) who granted for Porteous a reprieve of six weeks. Official notification of this reached Edinburgh on 2 September, six days before Porteous had been due to hang. On 4 September, the Lord Justice-Clerk wrote to the Duke of Newcastle: "This Act of Her Majesty's Royal mercy ... meets with almost a general approbation, especially among those of the higher rank and greatest distinction. And the few who grumble are only of the meaner sort".[22] Mean they may have been, but few they were not.

In the taverns and coffee-houses of Edinburgh, rumour was rife of a plan to murder Porteous. On 7 September, Captain Lind of the Town Guard again warned Lord Provost Alexander Wilson about this and, though the Provost planned to reinforce the Town Guard the next day (the original execution day), he put no great store by the rumours. Neither indeed did Porteous himself, who dined in his Tolbooth cell that afternoon with one John Ure, who recalled him saying "he was no manner of Way affraid of any Mob and that if the Door was open'd to him he Would Venture to goe to the [Mercat] Cross with his cane alone in his hand".[23]

Also on 7 September, James Graham wrote to Lord Aberdour: "your Lordship weel knows no disturbance will be attempted here on account of Porteous's reprieve ... There's nothing of news stirring here but ane exceeding dead town."[24] That same night, it was to become an exceedingly lively town.

Shortly after 9 o'clock, a crowd began to gather in the western suburb of Portsburgh. They seized the drum from the burgh drummer's house, forcing his son to march with them, beating a call to arms. They took over the West Port, then, on the east, the Cowgate and Nether Bow Ports[25] (by which troops stationed in the Canongate might have entered), closing all the gates and, with small squads despatched to secure the Bristo and Potter Row Ports from outside interference, the main body, increasing in size all the time, then marched up the High Street to the Guard-house, whose soldiers they overpowered with ease, before seizing muskets and Lochaber axes.[26] Thus armed, they did not loot or rampage, but marched determinedly towards the Tolbooth. They were now 4,000-strong.

Meanwhile, in a Parliament Close tavern, Provost Wilson was quietly quaffing his claret when he was brought the distressing news. The obvious thing for him to do was to call out the troops from the castle, but he thought this required orders from General Moyle, who lived at Abbey Hill. So, instead of sending a messenger to the castle (where the troops were by now drawn up in readiness), he sent Patrick Lindsay M.P. to get orders from General Moyle.

Lindsay went directly to the Nether Bow but of course found it occupied by the mob. Feeling distinctly conspicuous, he dodged into a close to think for a bit. Then he decided to try the Potter Row Port, which he managed to get through while it was not properly secured by the mob, and so — after more circuitous plodding — arrived at Moyle's Abbey Hill mansion-house at fourteen minutes to eleven.

The General, however, even though he had already called out troops in the Canongate, refused to give any further orders unless he could see a magistrate's warrant. For, with the recent example of Porteous himself in mind, he was not keen to spill unauthorised blood. Thus there arose the absurd scenario of a mob rioting with impunity, while troops stationed in the Canongate to the east and the castle to the west stood by and did nothing.

Provost Wilson, in the meantime, had decided to do something himself. Summoning up his courage, he set off to face the mob, which he did for a few seconds, before scurrying back to Clerk's Tavern under a hail of stones and insults.

While all this was going on, Porteous must have been frantic. The mob battered at the mighty Tolbooth door for a full hour, before finally resorting to fire to break it down.

At half past eleven they were through and, after freeing 17 other prisoners (including the seven soldiers of the Guard arrested with Porteous [27] — thus indicating the personal nature of the vendetta), they seized their quarry and dragged him out.

Porteous was carried by the torch-bearing mob to the Grassmarket, via the West Bow, where a shop was broken into and a rope taken, with a guinea left in payment.[28] Then, being refused a final prayer, he was strung up from a dyer's pole, only to be let down again and his nightshirt tied about his head, while, according to one witness, "some of the mob [made] a proposal of cutting his ears out, and others proposed to geld him".[29]

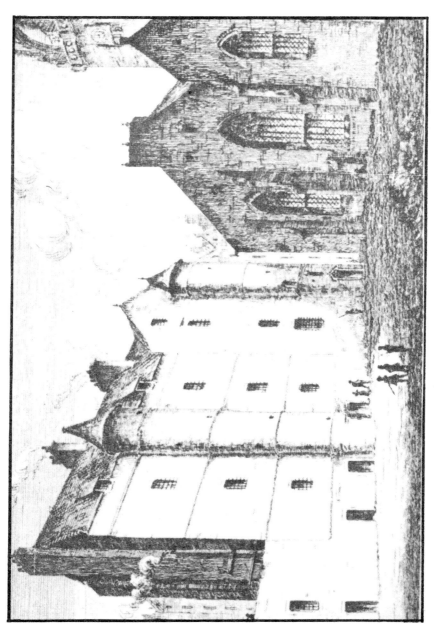

The Tolbooth of Edinburgh

They settled for hauling him up to hang again and, when his hands struggled to free the rope, they battered his right arm and shoulder with a Lochaber axe. Then they let him down again and beat him up some more before hauling him up for the third and last time. And when he had finally expired, the mob, as organised as when it began, scattered its weapons and disappeared off the streets. "Now," said one of them, "the Queen can wipe her backside with her reprieve."[30]

6. THE AFTERMATH

It was 5a.m. before Porteous's body was cut down. Having ventured forth at last, the magistrates found only a few malingerers, whom they arrested. Only one of these, William Maclauchline, footman to the Countess of Wemyss, was ever brought to trial. However, he was found to have been so drunk on the night that he could hardly have hung up his coat let alone a man, and so was acquitted by the unanimous vote of the jury. In fact, no one was ever caught and convicted. Whether from fear or solidarity, and despite big rewards for informers, almost nobody could be found to speak out and identify the rioters. Suspects were arrested and interrogated to no avail and when one Thomas Linnen, who *may* actually have played some part, was brought to trial in June 1737, he too was acquitted.[31]

The discipline of the riot and the unco-operative silence that ensued made the London authorities fear the worst. A succession of phantom Jacobites, Covenanters and fanatical clergymen was conjured up as having been behind the riot but, in the end, it was the whole town that went on trial. In April 1737, a bill was proposed in the House of Lords for abolishing the Town Guard and taking away the Nether Bow Port gates and for banning Lord Provost Wilson (by now in custody) from taking office anywhere in the country. Despite strenuous opposition from the Duke of Argyll and others normally loyal to the establishment, the bill was passed in the Lords.

But by the time it came to the House of Commons, it was widely felt that the whole long drawn-out business had got out of hand and the conviction had grown that, as the phrase had it, the innocent were being punished for not being guilty. In the end, the bill was watered down so that the city was just fined £2,000 to be paid to Porteous's grieving (?) widow, though Lord Provost Alexander Wilson was still barred from further office.

Unfortunately, however, the matter rumbled on, thanks to a bill passed at the instigation of the Earl of Islay (Argyll's brother), whereby Scotland's clergymen were to read out from their pulpits on the first Sunday of every month an act promising the death sentence for absconding riot suspects (Thomas Linnen had been one such) and rewards for informers. This caused outrage in the Scottish church, always sensitive about its relations to the state, and led to ridiculous situations where ministers dismissed their congregations and read the proclamation to the empty pews.

On 28 June 1737 Alexander Wilson, the ex-Lord Provost freed from custody, returned to Edinburgh. Thousands lined the streets as the church bells rang out, bonfires were lit and a jubilant town defiantly celebrated.

POSTSCRIPT

On 31 August 1737, the Town Council passed an act, whereby "the Person or Persons who shall be hereafter found guilty, or Art and Part of throwing Stones, Mud, Dung, or other Garbage, at the Officers of the Law, City-guard or Common Executioner... shall... be whipt through the City by the Hand of the Common Hangman, and thereafter imprisoned for the Space of one Year."[32]

NOTES AND REFERENCES

1. Alexander Clerk, witness at the subsequent trial. See **CRIMINAL TRIALS illustrative of the tale 'The Heart Of Midlothian'**, Edinburgh, 1818, p.45. Scott's **THE HEART OF MIDLOTHIAN** is based on the Porteous Riot.

2. Wm. Roughead, **TRIAL OF CAPTAIN PORTEOUS**, Glasgow & Edinburgh, 1909, p. 3.

3. See, respectively, Edinburgh City Archives, Town Council Minutes (TCM) vol. 43; Roughead, op. cit. pp.9-10, citing the **NEWGATE CALENDAR** (1773), vol. III, p.22; Roughead p.17, citing **THE HISTORY OF THE WEST KIRK** (1829); TCM vol. 56 (also Bundle 40 (McLeod), nos. 27 &28).

4. Robert Thin, 'The Old Infirmary and Earlier Hospitals', **THE BOOK OF THE OLD EDINBURGH CLUB**, vol. 15, 1927, p.145.

5. op. cit. pp. 20-21.

6. The proceedings are recorded in **CRIMINAL TRIALS** (see 1. above).

7. The *Caledonian Mercury* 12 April 1736, quoted in Roughead, p.71 (cf. Alexander Carlyle's account in his **AUTOBIOGRAPHY**, ed. John Hill Burton, London & Edinburgh, 1910, pp.38-40).

8. National Library of Scotland (NLS), Saltoun Papers, MS 17509, f.1.

9. *Authentic Extract of the* PROCEEDINGS *in the* TRIAL *of Captain John Porteous*, London, 1737 (evidence of defence witness, Alexander Thomson).

10. ibid., (Information for John Porteous).

11. ibid., (Information for John Porteous).

12. ibid., (Information for John Porteous).

13. In the precognition, if we discount those with irrelevant information and those concerned with the aftermath - clearing the bodies - 39 witnesses, 19 of whom also gave evidence at the trial, saw Porteous fire; 17, eight of whom gave evidence at the trial, heard Porteous order the men to fire, and a further two, one of whom was called, heard him threaten that his men would fire (NLS, Saltoun Papers, MS 17509, ff. 1-25).

14. See, respectively, *Authentick Extract...* , defence witness no. 13; ibid., prosecution witness no. 6; precognition, NLS, Saltoun Papers, MS17509, f. 23.

15. In the precognition, virtually no-one offered positive (that is, positively negating) evidence on Porteous's behalf. Fourteen of his own men — some to be arrested themselves — gave statements: five said Porteous fired first, two of those and two more heard Porteous give orders to fire, three heard nothing of the sort, and a futher four heard somebody — they could not say whom — shout 'Fire!' In all this, it is salutary to note that not one woman (many of whom must have been present — one was killed and at least two wounded) was required to give evidence at either the precognition or the trial.

16. op. cit. p.56.

17. See, respectively, *Authentick Extract...*, prosecution witnesses nos. 7 & 11; defence witnesses nos. 1 & 8; precognition, Saltoun Papers, op. cit., f. 11.

18. Saltoun Papers, op. cit., f. 15.

19. Evidence to the subsequent House of Lords enquiry, quoted Roughead, op. cit., p.44.

20. Hew Dalrymple, letter to Lord Aberdour, 18 Aug. 1736, Scottish Record Office(SRO), Morton Papers, GD 150/3480/10.

21. *A Memorial For The People Of Scotland*, Dublin, 1737, p.4. Like the earlier mentioned *Life And Death Of Captain Porteous*, this had an anonymous, and similarly vituperative, author. It can be found in the Central Public Library's Porteous collection.

22. quoted in Roughead, op. cit., p.69.

23. A copy of Ure's statement can be found in Edinburgh City Archives, bundle 40 (McLeod), no.56.

24. SRO, Morton Papers, GD 150/3480/24.

25. The 'ports' were gateways (sometimes set in beautiful edifices such as the Nether Bow), which afforded passage through the town walls. (From the French *Porte*).

26. Only 15 soldiers were on duty in the entire town that evening and these, after the events of 14 April, were not carrying firearms.

27. Another eight were held in the Canongate Tolbooth. One of these

escaped in July 1736 and the rest were released the following November.

28. The shop still exists — no. 89 West Bow/Victoria Street, 'Ye Olde Curiosity Shoppe'.

29. 'Proceedings in the Trial of William MacLauchlane', in **CRIMINAL TRIALS**, op. cit., p.305.

30. See *Letter Giving A Contemporary Account Of The Murder Of Captain John Porteous*, Sept. 1736, published in Roughead, op. cit., appendix IV, p.242.

31. Useful analyses of the mob's likely ringleaders can be found in 'The Porteous Riot, 1736', in *History Today* (April 1972) and in 'The Porteous Riot: A Study of the Breakdown of Law and Order in Edinburgh, 1736-1737', in the *Journal Of The Scotish Labour History Society*, no.10. June 1976, both by H.T. Dickinson & K.J. Logue.

32. A copy of the Act can be found in Central Public Library's Edinburgh Room, ref. qYDA 1860.736 [42787]

GUIDE TO SOME SOURCES

There are four main *loci* of research in Edinburgh. These are:

1. The Edinburgh Room, Central Public Library: contains 49 items grouped around the ref. no. YDA 1869.736; 15 of these, including the *Authentick Extract* of the trial, the *Life And Death Of Captain Porteous,* and the *Memorial For The People Of Scotland,* are bound in one volume called **PORTEOUS MOB PAMPHLETS I**; some of these are reproduced, with three other documents (a poem, an Act of Council, and a speech by the Duke of Argyll), in a collection called **THE TRIAL OF CAPTAIN PORTEOUS; PORTEOUS MOB PAMPHLETS II** has 11 items concerning the Act For Bringing To Justice The Murderers of Captain Porteous (which ministers had to read out every month); *The Genuine Tryal Of Capt. John Porteous,* petition of Queen Caroline, a contemporary account of the riot, the *Life And Death*, and a letter concerning the riot are brought together in one volume at YDA 1860.736 [42813]; proceedings in the Wilson-Hall-Robertson Porteous and MacLauchlane trials are reproduced in **CRIMINAL TRIALS illustrative of...** **'The Heart of Midlothian'** (Edin., 1818), ref. YPR 5317H [43381].

2. Edinburgh City Archives (currently located on level one of the City Chambers): apart from the Town Council Minutes, there are many items — including the *Authentick Extract*, the precognition letters, Acts, Tolbooth accounts etc. - tied together in Bundle 40 (McLeod) and several more in Bundles 160 & 161 (Moses).

3. The National Library of Scotland, South Reading Room (Manuscripts): various papers & letters can be found in MSS. 215 (ff.10-12), 580 (no.406), 591 (no.1798), 874 (ff.497, 522), 901 (ff.95-100), 2980 (f.27), 3112 (f.9) & 16565 (no.239); MS. 17509, Saltoun Papers, is the richest source, containing not only the precognition and *Authentick Extract*, but also the Porteous trial notes of Lord Milton, the presiding judge.

4. The Scottish Record Office, Register House: the Morton Papers, GD 150/3480, contain 29 letters and papers relating to the riot and subsequent parliamentary enquiry; other material can be found in the Clerk of Penicuik Collection, GD 18/3222 & 3223, and in the State Papers (Scotland), Sept.-Nov. 1736, RH2/4/335.

Apart from these primary sources, William Roughead's **TRIAL OF CAPTAIN PORTEOUS** (Glasgow & Edinburgh, 1909), which reproduces texts of many original documents, is essential reading. The **AUTOBIOGRAPHY** of Alexander Carlyle (1722-1805) has valuable first-hand accounts of both Robertson's escape and the events of 14 April, 1736. 'The Porteous Riot, 1736', in *History Today* (April 1972) and 'The Porteous Riot: A Study of the Breakdown of Law and Order in Edinburgh, 1736-1737', in the *Journal Of The Scottish Labour History Society,* no.10, June 1976, both by H.T. Dickinson & K.J. Logue, analyse the nature of the mob and the political implications of the riot. The Edinburgh Room has a useful collection of latter-day press cuttings on the Town Guard (ref. YHU8198T). Every Scot has, of course, read Scott's **HEART OF MIDLOTHIAN**. Mollie Hunter's **THE LOTHIAN RUN** is another novel set in 1736 with Porteous in the background, and is published in Canongate's excellent 'Kelpie' series for children.